Artificial Intelligence, Analog Soul

Nathan Apostle

Published by The Literary Banana, 2025.

ARTIFICIAL INTELLIGENCE, ANALOG SOUL

First edition. July 16, 2025.

ISBN: 979-8231326716

Written by Nathan Apostle.

Table of Contents

Introduction – AI Is Not a Magic Box

Let's get one thing straight: the AI is not going to write your novel for you. Sorry. I know. That sucks. But also—it's kind of amazing. Because what it can do is pretty wild, once you stop expecting it to hand you the next Dune and start using it like the supercharged creative assistant it was meant to be.

Think of AI like an incredibly fast, somewhat confused intern with a PhD in Everything and the memory of a goldfish. It's brilliant, but it needs your direction. It's powerful, but it's not psychic. And it definitely won't save your project from bad ideas, lazy storytelling, or plot holes you could fly a spaceship through.

This little book is here to show you how to get the most out of AI without losing your creative voice in the process. We'll cover what it's great at (outlining, idea bouncing, rewriting, pretending to be Hemingway for your opening paragraph), and what it's not so great at (emotional nuance, long-term consistency, understanding your subtext, remembering what you told it six minutes ago).

We'll also take a look at the current crowd of AI writing tools—like ChatGPT (hi there), Claude, Gemini, and others—and explain what you can do with the free versions versus paid or API tools. Spoiler: You can do a lot with free. But if you want the memory span of something better than a caffeinated squirrel, you might want to upgrade.

Finally, one important truth: if you feed it garbage, it gives you robot garbage back. Good prompts matter. Good ideas matter. You matter. AI isn't magic—it's a mirror. It reflects your intention, your craft, and your clarity. So, sharpen those things. Then let it help you write your damn book.

Chapter 1: Don't Be a Thief – 'Original Ideas Only, Please and Thank You'

Before we dive into prompts and plots and that one character who keeps turning into an orphaned assassin for no reason... let's talk about the very first rule of writing with AI:

Don't steal.

Now, maybe you're thinking, "I would never!" And I believe you. Mostly. But the line between "inspired by" and "copy-pasted from someone else's brain" can get a little blurry—especially when you're using a tool trained on the internet, and your prompt sounds suspiciously like Write me a story like Harry Potter but with dinosaurs and steampunk.

Let's be clear: if you're using AI to remix existing material and slap your name on it without making it your own, you're not a writer—you're a very lazy thief.

So What Counts as Stealing?

Asking AI to "write a novel in the style of [famous author]" = okay, within reason, but still sketchy.

Asking AI to write that author's actual plot, with different names = nope, illegal and creatively sad.

Copy-pasting long chunks of someone else's book to "feed into the AI" so it can "continue it for you" = criminal behavior with extra steps.

Using the AI to riff on public domain works or well-known tropes = totally fine, welcome to the party.

Publishing an AI-generated sequel to The Hunger Games and pretending it's original = see you in court, probably.

How to Check If Your Idea or Title Is Already Taken

Before you fall in love with your brilliant idea for a dystopian thriller about teenagers who fight each other on live TV... do some checking. You don't want to spend six months polishing The Carnage Bowl only to discover The Blood Trials, The Savage Games, and Hunger Fest already exist and are doing it better.

Start with these:

- Google it (seriously, most people skip this)
- Amazon search (see what books pop up with similar titles or blurbs)
- Goodreads (you'll see reader feedback on similar concepts—some of it scathing)
- US Copyright Office database (if you're in the U.S.)
- ISBN search at isbnsearch.org (to see if your title already has a literary twin)

If someone else has your title, it's not the end of the world—but it is a sign you might want to tweak or reframe it. You want to stand out, not get buried in a pile of samey clones.

Tools for Checking Plagiarism (Yes, Even If You Didn't Mean To)

AI makes it easy to accidentally mimic existing text. You type a vague prompt, and boom: it spits out something that sounds amazing—because it may have seen it before.

To protect yourself:

- Grammarly Premium – includes a solid plagiarism checker.
- Originality.AI – checks both plagiarism and ai-generated content.
- Copyscape Premium – checks for duplicated content across the internet, popular with indie authors and content marketers.
- QuillBot – integrated with rewriting/paraphrasing tools.
- Scribbr (Turnitin-powered) – academic gold standard, overkill for your fiction novel.
- Others: Quetext, Plagscan.
- Google Search – paste a few sentences in quotes and see what shows up.

You don't have to obsess over this. Just make sure your core material isn't lifted from some poor author who already spent three years in a caffeine-fueled fog birthing it into the world.

Disclaimer: Copying Another Author's Style

"Just Because You Can Doesn't Mean You Should"

So, you fed your AI a prompt like:

"Write this in the style of Neil Gaiman meets Stephen King meets a Red Bull-fueled Jane Austen."

Technically? That's not illegal.

Morally? It's a little... sweaty. Like showing up at a costume party wearing someone else's skin. Yes, style isn't copyrightable. But voice is intimate. Hard-earned. And mimicking a living author too closely can come off as lazy, creepy, or both.

In Summary:

- It's okay to be inspired by your favorites.
- It's not okay to carbon-copy them and slap your name on it.
- Respect the work. Find your own weird, wonderful voice. We promise it's in there.
- Remember, writing isn't karaoke. You don't win points for sounding exactly like the original—just for being unforgettable in your own key.

Pro Tip: Start with Your Weird Little Angle

The best way to avoid accidental plagiarism? Be weird. Be specific. Start from your obsessions, your vibe, your secret notebook full of cursed plot ideas. That's where the real originality lives.

Don't ask the AI to give you a "generic fantasy plot." Instead, try:

"Help me brainstorm a fantasy novel where the magic system is based on fermentation, and the villain is a sentient sourdough starter."

Now that's a story no one else is writing. Probably for good reason.

So, before we move on to the fun stuff—prompts, outlines, worldbuilding—take a moment. Lock in your idea. Check the title. Do the legwork. Respect other creators. And give the AI a fighting chance to help you build something truly original.

Next up: your AI co-author's a genius. With short-term memory loss. Let's talk about how to work with that.

Chapter 1 Checklist: Keep It Original

Before You Write:

Did I Google my idea/title to see if it's already taken?

Did I search Amazon or Goodreads for similar books or concepts?

Did I check if my title is copyrighted or already published?

Am I starting from my own unique angle or obsession?

When Using AI:

Am I prompting for help—not for copying?

Am I avoiding "continue this exact text" unless it's mine?

Am I using public domain or original material to inspire, not clone?

After the AI Spits Something Out:

Did I run a quick plagiarism check (Grammarly, Copyscape, Quetext)?

Did I paste a suspiciously slick sentence into Google just to be safe?

Did I tweak, rewrite, or personalize the AI's draft in my own voice?

Big No-Nos:

Don't publish AI output that mimics copyrighted works

Don't reuse fanfiction or sequels unless it's parody or clearly transformative

Don't assume AI "makes it original" just because it changed the names

Bottom line: AI is here to help you be original—not to do crimes on your behalf.

Chapter 2: AI Has Dementia – 'Grandma Writes Like a Genius, but She Can't Remember Your Name'

Let's set the scene: You've just spent 45 minutes explaining your plot, your main character's tragic backstory, the rules of your fictional bee-powered magic system, and the exact tone you want for your novel— "lightly noir with a sprinkle of sapphic cottagecore."

Then, you type:

"Okay, now write the next scene."

And your beloved AI co-author responds like this:

"Sure! Here's a story about two completely new characters in a gritty sci-fi space casino using guns instead of bees."

That, dear writer, is AI memory in action.

AI Memory, or Lack Thereof

Think of AI like your incredibly smart, award-winning grandmother who can quote Shakespeare and do calculus in her head—but will also call you "Greg" even though your name is Maya, and you've told her seventeen times already.

In short: AI is brilliant. But it has the short-term memory of a particularly dazed goldfish.

Here's What That Means:

Free AI (like the free version of ChatGPT):

It remembers nothing. Every prompt is a fresh start. It doesn't know who you are, what you're writing, or what you said four messages ago unless you copy-paste it back in like a frantic court stenographer.

Premium AI (ChatGPT Plus, Claude Pro, Gemini Advanced):

Some versions do have session-based memory or even long-term memory (if you turn it on), but even then... don't get too comfortable. It might remember your protagonist is named "Jax," but forget what species they are, or that you said, "No more dream sequences, please."

Session Memory vs Persistent Memory:

Session memory = it remembers stuff during the chat but forgets once you close the tab or start over.

Persistent memory = it retains details across sessions—but it's limited, imperfect, and frankly a little nosy.

Some models let you "edit" what it remembers (cool), but it's like editing a foggy scrapbook with post-it notes.

How to Work Around It Like A Pro

You don't give a genius with dementia a high-stakes solo writing gig—you give them structure, reminders, and a big-font notebook labeled "IMPORTANT THINGS."

Here's what that looks like for you:

Save Your Key Info Outside the App

Character sheets – basic stats, voice, goals, relationships, quirks

Worldbuilding summaries – rules of the world, vibe, magic systems, tech, etc.

Tone & style guides – is this dark and poetic? Satirical and punchy? "Wes Anderson with zombies"?

Your outline or beat sheet – even just rough chapter goals

Paste these back in as needed. Better yet, create a standard prompt:

"Remember this info for our project. Refer to it often."

Then drop your notes.

Bonus tip: Create a reusable doc or text file with all your key info. That way, you're not reinventing your own wheel every time the AI forgets how wheels work.

Think of It Like This:

You're co-writing a novel with a genius who has memory loss. They're fast, articulate, occasionally brilliant—but they forget everything you said 30 seconds ago and sometimes invent new cousins for your protagonist mid-scene.

You wouldn't yell at Grandma. You'd repeat the important stuff. You'd be patient. You'd keep notes. Same here.

Bottom line:

AI isn't your all-knowing book genie—it's your eccentric, brilliant writing partner with no short-term memory. You can work with that. Just bring a notebook and a little grace.

Next up: Backups, disasters, and the magic of hitting "Save."

Chapter 2 Checklist: AI Memory Survival Guide

Understand the Memory Basics

Free AI = Goldfish memory. It forgets everything between sessions.

Premium AI = Slightly better goldfish. Can remember some stuff across chats.

Session memory = short-term memory for one chat window.

Persistent memory = long-term-ish memory (if enabled), but still needs reminders.

Create & Maintain Your Own Brain Backup

Character sheets saved outside the app

Worldbuilding notes or "universe rules" file

Voice, tone, or style guides in your own words

An outline or scene tracker you can reuse

Use Smart Prompts to Reboot Memory

"Here's context for our story—please remember this while writing."

Keep prompts handy so you're not rewriting setup every time.

When the AI forgets: don't panic. Just re-paste and move on.

Golden Rule:

Treat your AI like a genius with dementia. Be patient. Keep notes. Don't expect it to remember your name—or your main plot twist—without help.

Chapter 3: AI on a Trip – 'No, not to New Zealand. When Your AI Seems Like It Has Eaten Shrooms'

So, you're writing nonfiction. Or reality-based fiction. Or just anything that involves names, dates, quotes, locations, or, you know... verifiable facts. And you think, "Hey, I'll just ask my AI buddy to summarize it for me! That's fast! Efficient! Safe!" Except it's not.

Because sometimes your AI isn't just wrong—it's weirdly confident and weirdly wrong, like a college roommate who insists the moon landing happened in 1982 and that dolphins speak Portuguese.

Welcome to the world of AI hallucinations. (Yes, that's the real term. Yes, it's terrifying.)

What Even Is a Hallucination?

In AI-speak, a "hallucination" is when the model makes stuff up. Not in a cute, creative writing way. In a "here's a fake Harvard study from 1997 that never existed but sounds real and now you've accidentally plagiarized a ghost" kind of way. It might:

- Attribute quotes to the wrong people
- Invent articles or books
- Mix up timelines
- Reference sources that were used during training but aren't public
- Pull facts from alternate dimensions

Think of it like this: your AI is a very eager intern who desperately wants to be helpful, but it was raised by Wikipedia and bold lies.

How to Spot AI on Shrooms

Some red flags your AI is hallucinating:

- It cites a study with no author, no date, and no journal
- It gives oddly specific numbers but can't explain where they came from
- It says something like, "According to a 2021 article in The Economic Review..." and no such journal exists
- You try to Google it and get nothing but yoga pants ads

If you can't verify it in under 60 seconds, don't trust it.

How to Fact-Check Without Losing Your Will to Live

1. Google Is Still Your Friend

Search the claim or quote directly. If it only appears on shady websites or AI forums... nope.

2. Use Real Databases When Possible

JSTOR, PubMed, Google Scholar, or even your local library's digital resources. Yes, libraries still exist. They even let you in without a password.

3. Ask for Sources—Then Actually Check Them

You can prompt:

"Give me five real, verifiable sources on [topic], with working links and publication info."

(Then verify them like a suspicious librarian.)

4. Use AI to Summarize, Not Verify

Once you've found a legit article, then use AI to summarize it, translate the jargon, or turn it into bullet points for your outline.

Trust it to organize. Not to tell the truth.

How to Minimize Hallucinations in the First Place

- Be specific. Vague prompts = confident nonsense.
- Avoid asking for "facts" or "data" without follow-up.
- Use versioned, reputable models (Pro versions of GPT, Claude, Gemini).
- Turn on plugins/tools that allow for real-time web browsing (if available).
- Always keep a skeptical brain on. Just because it said it in a British accent doesn't make it true.

Bonus Reminder: Still Don't Plagiarize, You Beautiful Disaster

This should go without saying, but here we are. If AI gives you a quote, an article, or even a paragraph that sounds a little too polished—run it through a plagiarism checker. Cite your sources. Rewrite with your voice. If you wouldn't steal from Wikipedia with a ski mask on, don't do it here either.

Final Thought:

AI is great at assisting—not authoring. If you're writing anything rooted in truth, you are now the designated adult in the room. Congratulations. Your prize is critical thinking and avoiding lawsuits.

Next up: Backups, disasters, and the magic of hitting "Save."

Chapter 4: Save, Save, Save – 'AI Will Ghost You—Backups Won't'

Look, I don't want to alarm you, but one day—without warning—your AI is going to ghost you.

Maybe the browser crashes. Maybe your free-tier chat hits its token limit and wipes your history. Maybe the server hiccups and your beautifully worded third act disappears into the digital abyss like a tragic Shakespearean side character.

And that's when you'll wish you listened to this chapter.

Why Saving Matters More Than You Think

Writing with AI feels fast. One second, you're spitballing, worldbuilding, the next you've got a two-page monologue from your villain that absolutely slaps. You're in the zone. You think: "I'll just keep going and clean it up later."

Until later never comes. Because the chat resets.

Or you forget to copy it.

Or you accidentally close the tab to check if raccoons can legally be emotional support animals. (Answer: it depends on your state.)

So, here's the deal: If you love your words, save your words.

Tools for Not Losing Your Mind (or Manuscript)

You don't need to be fancy. You just need a system. Here are a few tools that won't ghost you:

Google Docs

- Free, cloud-based, autosaves every keystroke.
- Great for quick drafts, shared edits, and yelling "WHY DID YOU DELETE THAT SCENE?!" at your future self.

Notion

- A productivity nerd's dream.
- Great for organizing outlines, character bios, timelines, and worldbuilding all in one place.
- A little overkill if all you want is a single doc, but glorious for complex projects.

Obsidian

- Local-first, markdown-powered, link-everything-to-everything chaos machine.
- Ideal if your brain operates like a conspiracy board.
- Nerdy, but delightful once you get the hang of it.

Scrivener

- Writer-friendly, built for long-form work.
- Scene cards, chapter folders, corkboard view—it's the writing cabin of your dreams.
- Downside: It costs money and has a learning curve shaped like El Capitan.

GitHub (Yes, Really)

- Best if you're collaborating, version-controlling like a boss, or just want to flex.
- Bonus: You'll feel very cool saying, "Oh yeah, I'm pushing my latest chapter to Git."

Naming Conventions

(AKA "Draft_Final_FINAL_revised_REALfinal_v3" Syndrome)

If you've ever had a folder full of documents that all say final but none of them are... hi, welcome.

Let's fix that:

Use Smart, Boring File Names

- Novel_Ch06_FirstDraft_2025-06-09
- Novel_Ch09_BackupBeforeAIWreckedIt
- Just be consistent. Use dates or version numbers you can sort.

Bonus tip: Use folders. Keep your drafts, notes, outlines, and AI output separated like grumpy roommates. This will save your life in edits.

Assume Nothing Is Safe

AI doesn't autosave for you. It doesn't keep permanent logs. And if you think "Oh, I'll just scroll up and copy it later"—that's adorable.

Copy it now. Paste it now. Save it now.

Pro Tip: Save Even the Weird Stuff

Sometimes the AI will spit out a scene that makes no sense—but has one killer line. Or a side character you didn't ask for, but kinda love. Save it in a "junk drawer" doc. You never know when inspiration will Frankenstein itself into greatness.

Next up: how to talk to the AI in a way that gets results. (Spoiler: it's all in the prompt.)

Chapter 4 Checklist: Backup Like a Boss

Step 1: Assume AI Will Forget You Exist

Did I copy the AI's output before refreshing or closing the tab?

Did I save anything good (or weird-but-interesting bits) to my docs?

Did I scream into the void when I forgot?

Step 2: Choose Your Weapon(s)

Google Docs – For fast, flexible, auto-saving goodness

Notion – For organizing all the things

Obsidian – For linking your madness into brilliance

Scrivener – For novel-first, long-form mastery

GitHub – For version control gods and show-offs (no shame)

Step 3: Get Organized or Get Lost

Use version numbers or date stamps like: Draft_2025-06-07

Keep a folder just for AI-generated content

Create a "Junk Drawer" file for weird gems and happy accidents

Avoid file names like "Final_final_USETHISoneREALLY"

Golden Rule:

If it matters, save it in two places—minimum.

(Cloud + local. Or cloud + email. Or cloud + handwritten on a napkin. Whatever works.)

Chapter 5: It's All in the Prompts – 'Talk to It Like a Teammate Who's a Bit Too Literal'

AI is not magic. It's not psychic. And it sure as hell isn't subtle. If you treat it like a creative partner, great things can happen. If you treat it like a mind-reader, it will confidently hand you garbage and expect a thank-you.

Think of AI Like an Intern with Infinite Knowledge and Zero Intuition

It's like working with that one overly helpful teammate who does exactly what you ask for—even if what you asked for makes zero sense. You say: "Write a witty romantic comedy."

It hears: "Please generate 1,000 words of two robots trading awkward puns while comparing spreadsheet formulas."

That's not its fault. It's yours. You need better prompts.

Good Prompts Are Specific, Structured, and Clear on Tone

✘ Bad:

"Write a cool story."

"Make it funny and serious and romantic but also dystopian and maybe include frogs."

This is like handing a toddler a grocery list written in emojis and expecting them to come back with dinner.

✓ Good:

"Write the opening scene of a cozy mystery set in a small-town bookstore. The tone should be witty and warm, like Knives Out meets Gilmore Girls. Introduce the main character: sarcastic but lovable, early 30s, secretly investigating a crime no one believes happened."

See the difference? You're giving it:

- A goal
- A tone
- A setting
- A vibe
- A character type
- A clear assignment

You're managing the AI. And you're doing great, sweetie.

Prompt Templates That Work Wonders

Use these like flexible mad libs. Customize as needed.

Idea Brainstorming:

"Give me 5 story ideas in [genre] that involve [theme/character conflict], with twist endings."

"List unusual settings for a [genre] novel that haven't been overdone."

Character Building:

“Create a character profile for a [age] [occupation] with a secret that could ruin their life. Include personality traits, voice quirks, and what they fear most.”

Dialogue Tweaks:

“Rewrite this scene to make the dialogue feel more natural, keeping the same meaning but adding humor and tension.”

“Make this conversation sound like two old friends catching up over drinks, one hiding something.”

Rewrite & Polish:

“Rewrite this paragraph to be tighter and punchier, like a noir detective voiceover.”

“Edit this for clarity but keep the tone casual and sarcastic.”

Style Mimicry:

“Write this in the style of a Wes Anderson script / a gothic Victorian letter / a Gen Z group chat meltdown.”

How to Accidentally Ruin Everything (Prompt Pitfalls)

Too Vague:

“Help me.”

The AI: “With what? Breathing? Taxes? Overcoming childhood trauma?”

Contradictory:

"Make this lighthearted and tragic and whimsical but also gritty realism."

It will try. You won't like it.

Too Long:

"Here is my 17-page plot synopsis, five different tone guides, six characters, and four competing instructions. Please write something."

AI will either implode or politely ignore half your input.

Pro tip: If your prompt looks like a college thesis or a nervous breakdown, cut it down. Break it into chunks.

Bottom Line: Prompt Like a Pro

Be clear. Be specific. Use examples.

Know what tone you want before you ask.

Don't treat AI like a wish-granting unicorn—it's a logic puzzle with a good vocabulary.

You're the brains of the operation. The AI is just very fast fingers.

Next up: What AI can help with (a lot), and what it absolutely cannot (sorry, it won't fix your motivation issues).

Chapter 5 Checklist: Prompt Like You Mean It

Know Who You're Talking To

AI is smart but not psychic. Be clear.

It's like an eager intern: fast, obedient, and occasionally clueless.

Manage expectations—you're the boss.

Good Prompt Rules

Be specific: what genre, what vibe, what goal?

Include tone cues (e.g., "light and sarcastic" or "dark and brooding").

Define the task clearly ("Write a scene," "List 5 ideas," "Edit for flow").

Give examples if needed.

If it messes up, it's okay—rephrase and try again.

Use These Prompt Templates

Brainstorm: "Give me 5 ideas in [genre] with a twist."

Characters: "Build a [flawed/wounded/funny] character with secrets."

Dialogue: "Rewrite this to feel more natural/snarky/emotional."

Rewrites: "Edit this for clarity but keep the voice casual."

Style: "Write like a [noir detective/gothic narrator/Gen Z texter]."

Avoid Prompt Landmines

Don't be vague: "Help me" won't get you far.

Don't mix 6 tones in one request. AI isn't a blender.

Don't overload: break long prompts into digestible steps.

Don't panic when it fails—refine, retry, repeat.

Golden Rule:

Treat your prompt like an order at a strange restaurant. If you're vague, you'll get something weird with capers.

Chapter 6: What AI Can Do for You – 'Not a Ghostwriter, But a Great Assistant'

Let's get one thing straight:

AI is not going to write your novel for you.

(Unless you want something that reads like a robot fanfiction of a tax manual.)

But if you treat it like your creative sidekick—a caffeinated intern with an infinite idea bank and zero ego—then you, my friend, are in for a treat.

This chapter is your menu of what AI can do for you. And spoiler: it's a lot.

1. Brainstorming Titles and Premises

Struggling to name your novel something other than Untitled.docx? Just ask AI for 10 snappy title ideas based on your genre, theme, or vibe.

Example:

"Give me 10 thriller titles about a rogue AI and economic collapse."

You'll get things like Zero Balance, Protocol 404, or Your Bank Account Has Been Deleted.

(Okay maybe not that last one, but someone should write it.)

Also works for plot prompts, hook lines, and "what if?" scenarios. You bring the seed, AI throws water and sunlight on it.

2. Worldbuilding and Setting Ideas

Want a futuristic Tokyo-Mars hybrid with underwater trains and sentient vending machines? AI has your back.

Need names for five different medieval taverns and the secret society behind them? You got it.

You can ask for:

Geography, customs, and cultures

Historical events (real or invented)

Cool setting twists ("What if this town has no clocks?")

Basically, AI can fill in the blanks on your weird little world so you can focus on making it sing.

3. Character Development and Arcs

Tired of making your fifteenth protagonist "a sarcastic loner with a dark past"?

Let AI help you shake things up. Prompt it like:

"Give me 3 flawed but likable characters for a sci-fi heist story."

"Suggest an emotional arc for a villain who thinks they're the hero."

Also great for side characters, love interests, or your favorite: that one comic relief guy who absolutely dies in Chapter 12.

4. Outlining (Yes, With Structure!)

AI knows the classics. Ask it to break your novel into:

- Save the Cat beats
- Hero's Journey steps
- Three-act structure
- Seven-point story arc
- Dan Harmon's Story Circle

You don't have to follow any of them religiously, but getting a structured starting point is way better than staring into the void yelling, "What happens in Act 2?!"

5. Dialogue Help (AKA Banter Polish)

- AI doesn't always nail dialogue on the first try, but it can definitely:
- Rephrase clunky lines
- Adjust tone (snarkier, softer, more awkward, etc.)
- Add subtext or tension
- Cut down the waffle

Prompt like:

"Make this sound like two old friends who are starting to suspect each other."

"Punch this up with dry humor, like a Taika Waititi script."

It's not Aaron Sorkin, but it's not bad either.

6. Style and Tone Matching

Want your scene to feel like a gritty noir? A whimsical fairytale? A Gen Z rant?

AI's got range.

Copy in a paragraph and say:

"Rewrite this in the style of X."

or

"Make this sound more like Neil Gaiman meets Douglas Adams after two espressos."

It won't be perfect—but it'll get you 80% there fast.

7. Summarizing Your Own Rambling

Wrote 2,000 words of chaotic brainstorming and don't remember what you were trying to say?

Paste it into AI and ask:

"Summarize this into 3 key plot points."

or

"Make this mess readable for future-me."

It'll politely clean up after your creative tornado.

8. Generating Marketing Copy

AI can help you write:

- Back cover blurbs
- Query letters
- Taglines
- Elevator pitches
- "Why this book?" summaries for agents

It'll sound like a mix between a book blogger and a PR intern—which, honestly, is what you need.

9. Cover Concepts

AI can help describe the vibe you want to a designer or an AI image generator. Try:

"Describe a cover design for a romantic thriller set on a space station, with retro neon colors and a noir feel."

It'll spit out some surprisingly vivid ideas. You'll still need a human eye (or a prompt-savvy image generator), but you won't be starting from scratch.

AI can generate a cover for you but be aware that some publishers frown upon this or strictly prohibit it (see Chapter 8). And if you want to include art or images in your book, it is best to create it yourself or hire a starving artist.

AI Is Your Assistant, Not Your Boss

Remember: you still do the thinking. AI just saves you time, energy, and a few dozen existential breakdowns.

Treat it like a very enthusiastic assistant who can draft ten versions of something while you eat snacks and feel clever.

Up next: the things AI can't do—like invent your voice, finish your draft for you, or hold your hand when you spiral at 2 a.m.

Chapter 6 Checklist: What AI Can Do for You

Brainstorming Help

Ask for titles, plot ideas, or "what if?" scenarios

Generate alternate versions of your core concept

Explore new angles you hadn't considered (or feared)

Worldbuilding and Setting

Get location names, quirks, and histories

Invent cultural norms, slang, tech, or taboos

Ask "what's weird about this place?" and roll with it

Character Development

Build full profiles: goals, flaws, fears, quirks

Flesh out arcs (e.g., redemption, downfall, growth)

Develop side characters who aren't just cardboard cutouts

Outlining with Structure

Request outlines using Save the Cat, Hero's Journey, etc.

Break messy story ideas into clear beats

Experiment with pacing and structure (without crying)

Dialogue Polish

Rewrite lines for humor, tension, or authenticity

Adjust tone (e.g., sarcastic, sincere, sinister)

Inject subtext without writing a soap opera

Style + Tone Mimicry

Match or imitate styles (real authors, genres, vibes)

Translate dull prose into something alive

Use to test new narrative voices (and keep the good ones)

Summarizing Chaos

Clean up brainstorm dumps

Extract core ideas from 2,000-word rambles

Reorganize scattered notes into actual plans

Marketing Copy

Draft blurbs, elevator pitches, and hook lines

Create query letter drafts

Polish "about the author" bios that don't sound like hostage notes

Cover Art Prompts

Describe your book visually for an artist or AI tool

Generate imagery ideas (mood, palette, symbolism)

Avoid the dreaded "guy standing in a misty alley again" cover trope

Reminder: AI is your assistant, not your author. You still have to make the creative decisions. But with this sidekick? You'll move a lot faster—and have a lot more fun doing it.

Chapter 7: What AI Can't Do – 'You're Still the Human Here, Sorry'

Look, AI is brilliant. It's like having a trivia nerd, copy editor, and caffeine-fueled intern rolled into one glowing screen. But at the end of the day, there are some things—big things—it just can't do. Not now. Maybe not ever.

That's where you come in. You, with your lived experience and chaotic little heart full of feelings. You're the soul of this book, not the software.

Let's talk about where the silicon brain ends and your messy, glorious humanity begins.

1. Make Real Emotional Connections

AI can simulate emotion. It can imitate "grief" or "longing" or "yearning" (ugh), but it doesn't feel any of that. You do. And that shows in your writing.

When a reader cries at your story, it's not because the AI nailed a metaphor—it's because you reached into something human and handed it to them on a page. That's you. That's your job. Don't outsource the soul.

2. Remember Your Entire Story

AI has the memory of a pigeon with a head injury.

Even the fancy premium models can only hold so much context in their little silicon brains. If you expect it to remember that your villain has a limp, a British accent, and a twin brother with a vendetta from four chapters ago—spoiler: it won't.

Solution? Save those details yourself. (See: Chapter 3. Or tattoo it on your hand.)

3. Write with Lived Experience

AI has read a billion books and blogs. But it has never:

- Sat in a waiting room dreading test results
- Fallen in love while waiting at a bus stop
- Lost a sibling
- Fought with its mom over Thanksgiving
- Been stuck in traffic with a baby screaming and no AC

It doesn't live. So, it can't write like it has.

Your weird, wonderful, painful, joyful human experience is what makes your writing ring true. Use that. Use you.

4. Spot Subtle Clichés

Sure, AI can detect when you use a cliché like "her eyes sparkled like diamonds." But deeper narrative clichés? Like "this is literally the same chosen one arc with different hair"?

Nope. It'll ride that formula train right off a cliff if you let it.

If your plot feels weirdly familiar or your twist is telegraphed from page one, you need to notice that. AI won't wave a red flag. It'll just keep going, smiling politely.

5. Tell You If Your Story Matters

Is your story saying something new? Does it hit people in the guts? Will it linger in a reader's brain two weeks after they finish?

AI has no idea. It can't tell what resonates. It doesn't read with a soul, only with syntax. It'll say your vampire time-loop romance is "compelling" because it recognizes the pattern—not because it cares.

You need test readers. You need honest feedback. You need... well, humans.

6. Take Creative Risks

AI plays it safe. It likes patterns, tropes, and comfortable genre norms. It will never say:

"What if the protagonist dies in Chapter 2 and the cat becomes the hero?"

It doesn't take creative leaps—it optimizes. And optimization kills originality if you're not watching.

If you want to break a rule, bend a genre, or invent a whole new narrative shape, that spark won't come from AI. It'll come from you, possibly while half-asleep in the shower or panicking at 2am. You know—writer magic.

Final Thought:

AI can help you write a story. It can't give it a soul.

Only you can make it worth reading.

Chapter 7 Checklist: What AI Can't Do

Emotional Resonance

Write scenes that make people cry, laugh, or text their ex

Tap into your lived emotion, not AI's synthetic guesswork

Infuse your story with real human nuance

Big-Picture Memory

Track plotlines across chapters manually

Keep character quirks and arcs consistent

Maintain story continuity outside the AI's short-term memory

Lived Experience

Write from your real-life joys, heartbreaks, failures, and wins

Ground your characters in human messiness

Add texture only actual life can teach you

Deeper Cliché Detection

Watch out for overused plot structures (not just lines)

Question tropes that feel "safe" or pre-packaged

Ask: "Have I read this story before with different names?"

Story Significance

Test if your story matters—ask human beta readers

Write from purpose, not just prompt

Aim for emotional impact, not algorithmic efficiency

Creative Risks

Break rules boldly (and on purpose)

Twist genres, blend tones, and make weird narrative choices

Remember: originality often looks risky before it looks genius

Sticky Note Summary:

If it feels too easy, too smooth, or too safe... check if the AI took the wheel. Then yank it back and drive like a human.

Chapter 8: Disclaimer on AI Publishing and AI Cover Art – 'No Free Rides: You Still Have to Be the Grown Up'

You've used AI to write, edit, and dream up your cover. Smart. But before you lean on it too hard—or let it do your taxes—know this:

1. KDP Requires Transparency

Amazon's Kindle Direct Publishing says: "If any text, images, or translations are AI generated (not just assisted), you must disclose it when uploading your book or edits". That means:

- AI-spun text or cover = disclose
- AI-suggested ideas or proofing = no disclosure needed

Amazon won't label your book "AI inside," but they will check for misuse—and limit how much you can publish daily.

2. IngramSpark & Others Might Flat-Out Reject AI Use

IngramSpark says they "may remove content ... created using automated means, including ... AI". Their goal: safeguard quality in bookstores everywhere.

Other platforms like Draft2Digital and Barnes & Noble have already purged junk AI-content or flagged suspicious uploads.

3. Why Transparency Matters

Because readers deserve honesty—and because hiding AI use can sink your Amazon account or make your print-run vanish.

Authors Guild, Jane Friedman, and others are pushing for clear AI labeling. Amazon listened—so did we.

How to Stay on the Right Side of the Rules

Use Case	KDP	IngramSpark/Others
AI-generated Cover	✓ Must disclose	✘ May reject or delist
AI-assisted COVER (tweaked)	✓ No disclosure needed	✘ Risky—test policies first
AI-generated TEXT	✓ Must disclose	✘ May reject entirely
AI-assisted TEST (edits, ideas)	✓ No disclosure needed	✓ Generally safe

In doubt? Label it. Or don't. But don't say you didn't know.

4. Cover Art & Copyright Landmines

AI-generated covers can look awesome—until the red flags pop up:

- They scrape from unknown sources
- They might mimic copyrighted art
- Amazon may reject or remove them

If you use AI for covers, pick tools that allow commercial use (like Adobe Firefly or Midjourney w/ license).

Better yet? Use AI for brainstorming and hire a designer for the final art.

Final Words (Your Adult Clause)

AI is amazing—but only if you treat it responsibly. Disclose when needed. Do not plagiarize. Stay transparent, legal, and reader-friendly.

Follow the rules—or at least don't blame us when the publishing police come knocking. You got this.

Chapter 9: Publish That Thing! – 'From Draft to Bestseller, or at Least to Amazon'

Congratulations. You've written a novel. Or a novella. Or a weird genre-fluid fever dream that's exactly 17,000 words and features a psychic corgi who solves cryptocurrency crimes. Whatever it is, you finished it.

Now comes the part where you show it to the world. Or at least try not to break out in hives while uploading it to a storefront.

Here's how to turn your AI-assisted masterpiece into a published product—using a few more smart AI tricks, and a couple hard-earned human decisions.

Step One: Pick Your Poison (aka Self-Publishing Platform)

There are a few main players in the indie publishing arena. Choose based on your goals, tolerance for formatting pain, and whether you enjoy customer support that ghosts you.

Kindle Direct Publishing (KDP)

- Most popular. Easy-ish. Amazon-only (unless you opt out of exclusivity).
- Great if you want instant access to millions of Kindle users.
- Caveat: Formatting can feel like ritual sacrifice.

Draft2Digital

- The chill middle child of publishing. Distributes to almost everyone including Amazon.
- Converts your Word doc into surprisingly decent ebook files (like magic, but without the goat).
- Auto-distributes to Apple Books, Kobo, Barnes & Noble, libraries, etc., without needing a PhD in EPUB.
- Bonus: Free to use. They just take a small cut from sales—no upfront cost, no drama.
- Great for wide distribution without wide headaches.

IngramSpark

- Better for print distribution (bookstores, libraries).
- Slower, pricier, and more professional-looking.
- Good for people who want paperbacks in actual shops and are allergic to Amazon.

Gumroad, Payhip, Ko-fi

- Sell direct to readers. Keep more money.
- Great for digital extras: bonus scenes, workbooks, early drafts.
- No built-in audience—you bring the traffic.

Pro tip: You can publish on all of them if you're not exclusive to Amazon's Kindle Unlimited. But maybe just start with one unless you enjoy spreadsheets and light suffering.

Let AI Be Your Publishing Assistant (Not Your Publicist)

Just because you're done writing doesn't mean you're done using AI. It still has some party tricks left. Let's exploit them.

Author Bio Writing

Can't describe yourself without sounding like a networking robot or a washed-up wizard? AI can help.

Prompt idea:

"Write a short author bio for a speculative fiction writer who loves coffee, cats, and conspiracy theories."

Refine it until it sounds like you, but, like, on a good day.

Formatting Your Manuscript

Use tools like Atticus, Reedsy, Vellum (Mac only), or even Google Docs export for basic EPUBs. Then ask AI:

"How should a novel be formatted for KDP print and Kindle?"

or

"Generate a clean manuscript template for a 60,000-word novel."

AI won't format it for you—but it can walk you through it, explain margins, and help fix weird heading issues.

SEO Descriptions & Keywords

You'll need a book description that doesn't suck and metadata that helps people find you.

Ask AI for:

- Compelling back-cover blurbs

- Keyword-rich descriptions
- Suggested keywords/categories for Amazon

Caveat: Run all keywords through KDP's search bar. If no one's searching "steampunk cozy horror romance," maybe don't use that.

Launch Plans & Marketing Drafts

AI can outline a launch timeline, write email newsletters, create social posts, and brainstorm giveaways. All without groaning like your writer friends. Prompt it with:

"Create a simple 3-week book launch plan for a debut fantasy novel, including email and social media ideas."

Adjust. Customize. Remove anything that sounds like it was written by a LinkedIn bot.

A Quick Word on AI Cover Design

Yes, AI art generators exist. Yes, they're fast, sometimes cool, and occasionally not cursed-looking. But there are risks.

Pros:

- Cheap or free
- Customizable on the fly
- Fast turnaround

Cons:

- Can look weird or uncanny if you're not careful
- May pull from copyrighted images—risking takedowns

- Some stores and publishers ban AI-generated covers (or require disclosure)

If you're going AI art, use tools that allow commercial use and don't scrape without permission (e.g., Adobe Firefly, Midjourney with terms checked, etc.). Better yet, hire a real artist who won't accidentally give your main character five fingers and a sixth growing out of their forehead.

Last Words: You Got This

Publishing isn't about being perfect. It's about being done, proud, and brave enough to hit "Upload." Whether you sell ten books to strangers or just one copy to your mom (thanks, Mom), the point is: you finished a novel.

That's already a huge deal.

And if you did it with AI? Cool. You still had to steer the ship, keep it on course, and survive the storm of your own self-doubt. That's what writers do.

Now get that book out there.

Chapter 9 Checklist: Getting Published with a Little Help (and a Lot of Sanity)

Choose Your Publishing Platform

KDP (Amazon) – Easy, massive reach, Kindle-focused

Draft2Digital – Easy, free formatting tool, wide distribution.

IngramSpark – Pro print distribution, more setup hassle

Gumroad/Ko-fi/Payhip – Sell direct, better royalties, DIY traffic

Consider exclusivity vs. wide distribution

Let AI Help with Pre-Pub Tasks

Draft your author bio in a tone that sounds like you (but cleverer)

Ask for back cover blurbs (then punch them up yourself)

Generate SEO keywords and categories

Create a launch timeline and email/social content

Format That Sucker

Use tools: Atticus, Reedsy, Vellum, Google Docs → EPUB

Ask AI how to format properly for each platform

Double-check margins, fonts, line spacing, chapter breaks

Cover Your Cover (Responsibly)

Decide: AI-generated or hire a designer?

If AI: Use tools that allow commercial use

Check for platform restrictions on AI art

Watch for creepy hands, haunted eyes, and "Did a robot draw this?" vibes

Launch & Promote

Use AI to brainstorm launch plans

Draft newsletter emails and teaser posts

Create a landing page or book link hub

Set up pre-orders or Day 1 promo if available

Appendix I – Choose Your Weapons

AI WRITING MODELS: Your Digital Writing Buddies (and Occasional Frenemies)

ChatGPT (OpenAI)

✓ Friendly, versatile, great at conversation and creativity

✘ Sometimes wanders off-topic or makes stuff up with confidence

Claude (Anthropic)

✓ Focuses on helpfulness and safety; pretty chill

✘ Less flashy; can be a bit too cautious or vague

Gemini (Google DeepMind)

✓ Powerful and growing fast; good at complex tasks

✘ Limited public access; sometimes feels like a work in progress

Jasper

✓ Tailored for marketing copy and creative writing

✘ Subscription-only; pricey for casual users

Writesonic

✓ Quick drafts, blog posts, and brainstorming help

✘ Can be repetitive and formulaic at times

Copy.ai

✓ Great for short-form content and catchy lines

✘ Not ideal for long, nuanced storytelling

FORMATTING TOOLS: Who's Gonna Make You Look Good on the Page?

Kindle Create

✓ Free and easy for KDP; auto-recognizes chapters

✘ Basic; zero flair; locked into Amazon's playground

Microsoft Word

✓ Everyone has it; total control with styles

✘ Can turn into formatting chaos if you sneeze wrong

Atticus

✓ Built for authors; beautiful exports for print/ebook

✘ Still in development; subscription model

Scrivener

✓ Great writing + compiling in one

✘ Formatting can be fiddly and feels like a secret level

Vellum (Mac only)

✓ Gorgeous formatting with zero pain

✘ Only works on Mac and isn't cheap

Reedsy Book Editor

✓ Free, web-based, and clean design

✘ Limited customization and needs internet

Adobe InDesign

✓ Industry-standard power tool

✘ Like flying a spaceship to make toast

Google Docs

✓ Great for collaboration and backups

✘ Terrible for professional formatting

Calibre

✓ Nerd-friendly ebook conversions

✘ Clunky interface; not great for first-time users

Plagiarism Checkers: Who Tattles Best?

Originality.AI

✓ Catches AI + plagiarism in one scan

✘ Might accuse you of being AI

Grammarly Premium

✓ Handy and built-in

✘ Surface-level checks only

QuillBot

✓ Integrated with rewriting tools.

✘ Monthly page limits.

Copyscape

✓ Trusted for web content

✘ Meh for long-form or print books

Scribbr (Turnitin)

✓ Super thorough

✘ Overkill. Expensive.

Quetext

✓ Clean interface, decent results

✘ Free version is just a demo

Plagscan

✓ Professional with source links

✘ More business than bookish

About the Author

Nathan Apostle is a fiction writer with a biochemistry degree, a questionable sense of direction, and a habit of falling down research rabbit holes that somehow lead to entire novels. A husband and father of two, he badly balances bedtime stories with plotting near-future thrillers and robot-fueled chaos. He's diving headfirst into the dark waters of self-publishing—wearing floaties, a snorkel, and a wildly unnecessary machete. This is either the beginning of something brilliant... or a very entertaining shipwreck. Either way, he's all in.

Dedication

For Bean, Goose, and Moose.

www.ingramcontent.com/pod-product-compliance
Lightning Source LLC
LaVergne TN
LVHW022026200926
848481LV00007B/2557